Tell Me WHY

HISTORY

Questions and Answers

by

Rebecca Phillips-Bartlett

BEARPORT PUBLISHING

Minneapolis, Minnesota

Credits
All images are courtesy of Shutterstock.com, unless otherwise specified. With thanks to Getty Images, Thinkstock Photo, and iStockphoto.

Cover – BNP Design Studio, danceyourlife, Ivan Iwanicki. 4 – Marti Bug Catcher. 5 –para827.6–7 – Inspiring, Net Vector, vladwel, the8monkey. 8–9 – JungleOutThere, Marnikus, Rick Partington, NotionPic, siriwat sriphojaroen, suwatwongkham. 10 –11 – Marti Bug Catcher, Tartila, Little.Kalu, Macrovector. 12–13 – Georgi Fadejev, Lexi Claus. 14–15 – Sabina Schaaf, Gaidamashchuk. 16–17 – jhorrocks, On Lollipops, Sergey_Accha, asantosg, Enkel. 18–19 – Hung Chung Chih, Katason, ONYXprj, Khosro. 20 –21 – Tartila, Dotidrop, the8monkey. 22– Flash Vector, nickfz. 23– DaleReardon, Rawpixel.

Bearport Publishing Company Product Development Team
President: Jen Jenson; Director of Product Development: Spencer Brinker; Managing Editor: Allison Juda; Associate Editor: Naomi Reich; Associate Editor: Tiana Tran; Art Director: Colin O'Dea; Designer: Elena Klinkner; Designer: Kayla Eggert; Product Development Assistant: Owen Hamlin

Library of Congress Cataloging-in-Publication Data is available at www.loc.gov or upon request from the publisher.

ISBN: 979-8-88916-395-4 (hardcover)
ISBN: 979-8-88916-400-5 (paperback)
ISBN: 979-8-88916-404-3 (ebook)

For more information, write to Bearport Publishing, 5357 Penn Avenue South, Minneapolis, MN 55419.

Contents

TELL ME WHY

There are many ways to learn about history. We could look at how people dressed or where they traveled. We could see what they had by visiting museums or even learn more by reading books!

QUESTION

What questions do you have about history?

The world today is very different from how it used to be. Some of the things people did in the past might seem strange. There are so many things about history that leave us wondering **WHY?**

WHY DO WE LEARN ABOUT THE PAST?

Throughout history, people have faced many problems. Learning how people in the past **solved** those problems can help us face our own issues today.

History is full of interesting stories. However, we should think carefully about how we learn about the past. Often, we are shown only one side of the story. Asking questions can help us see the bigger picture.

WHY AREN'T THERE DINOSAURS ANYMORE?

Most dinosaurs went **extinct** about 66 million years ago. Many scientists believe they were wiped out by an asteroid that crashed into Earth. It's thought the asteroid was more than 6 miles (10 km) wide. Other scientists think the dinos may have been killed by huge volcanic **eruptions**.

QUESTION

Which of these reasons do you think is most likely?

WHY DID KNIGHTS WEAR ARMOR?

Knights were a type of soldier. Many knights wore armor to protect themselves during battle. Some also used armor to show how important they were.

WHY DID PIRATES WEAR EYE PATCHES?

Scientists think eye patches helped pirates see in the covered parts of their boats. Human eyes take about 20 minutes to **adjust** to the dark. By leaving one eye in the dark all the time, pirates didn't have to waste time waiting to adjust. They could just switch their eye patch and go.

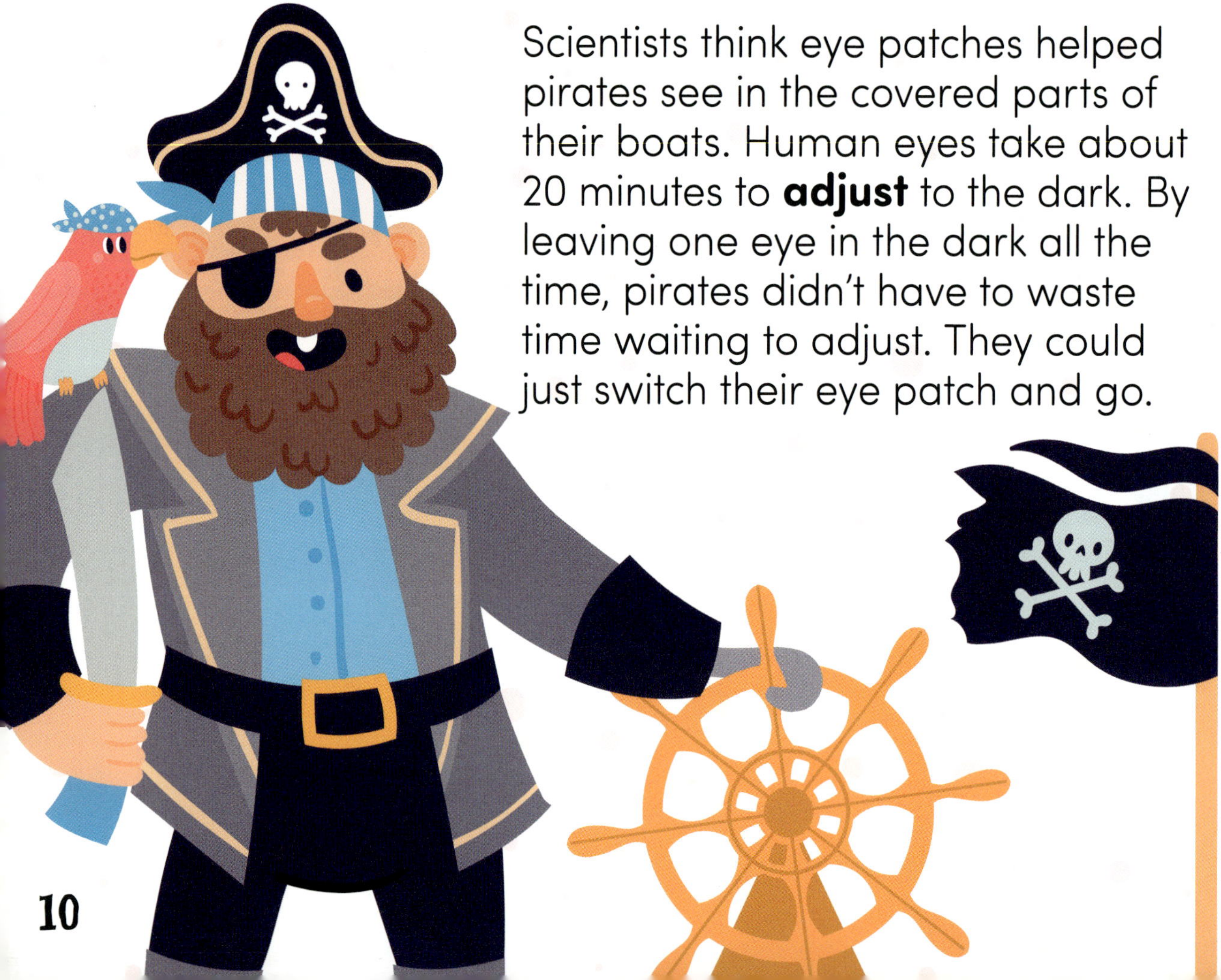

WHY DID ANCIENT EGYPTIANS MUMMIFY DEAD PEOPLE?

Ancient Egyptians believed that when a person died, they went to an **afterlife**. But to get there, the person's body needed to be prepared in a certain way. The **organs** had to be removed. Then, the body needed to be dried out and wrapped in bandages. This process was called mummification.

WHY DID THE PILGRIMS TRAVEL TO AMERICA?

The Pilgrims traveled from Europe to America in the early 1600s. At the time, everyone in England had to be part of the Church of England. But the Pilgrims wanted to follow a different religion. They set sail to find somewhere safe. The Pilgrims reached America in 1620.

WHY DID PLAGUE DOCTORS LOOK LIKE BIRDS?

In the late 1600s, an illness called bubonic plague killed many people across Europe. Back then, people thought **germs** were spread in bad-smelling air. Doctors wore beak-shaped masks that were filled with flowers to make the air smell nice.

FUN FACT

These masks had nose holes, so many doctors still breathed in germs and got sick.

WHY DID THE GREAT FIRE OF LONDON LAST SO LONG?

In 1666, a terrible fire burned London, England. It lasted for four days. The fire spread quickly because many buildings were made from wood. They were also very close together.

FUN FACT
The Great Fire of London started in a bakery on a road named Pudding Lane.

The city didn't have firefighters at the time. The people of London tried to put the fire out using simple tools, such as buckets of water. But that summer had been very dry and windy. This weather allowed the fire to spread faster than it could be put out.

WHY DID PEOPLE GO TO THE MOON?

FUN FACT

Neil Armstrong was the first person on the moon. He landed there in 1969.

In 1961, different countries began to compete to be the first to put a person on the moon. The United States wanted to show the world how good American **technology** was. Scientists spent the next few years working hard to send people to the moon.

WHY DID PEOPLE START USING FLAGS?

Thousands of years ago, people used **symbols** to show that they belonged to certain groups. The symbols were mainly on clothes, armor, and banners that soldiers carried into battles. By the 1700s, the symbols were put on flags like the ones we use today. They are used mostly to identify different countries.

WHY WAS THE GREAT WALL OF CHINA BUILT?

The people of ancient China built the Great Wall to protect themselves from **invading** armies. It was started by China's first **emperor**, Qin Shi Huang. The people of China continued to build this extremely long wall for the next 2,000 years.

WHY DO PEOPLE THINK VIKING HELMETS HAD HORNS?

People often think Vikings wore helmets with horns, but this probably isn't true. Scientists have found only one Viking helmet, and it didn't have horns! They think old stories about Vikings made up the part about horned helmets.

WHY DID THE SUFFRAGISTS FIGHT FOR THE RIGHT TO VOTE?

In many countries, people can vote to have a say in how things are done. However, it used to be only men who could do this. It wasn't until about 100 years ago that women in the United States gained the **right** to vote!

The suffragists were a group of women who fought for this right. They gave speeches, held parades, and even picketed outside the White House. Some women were arrested, but they did not stop until they had their message heard.

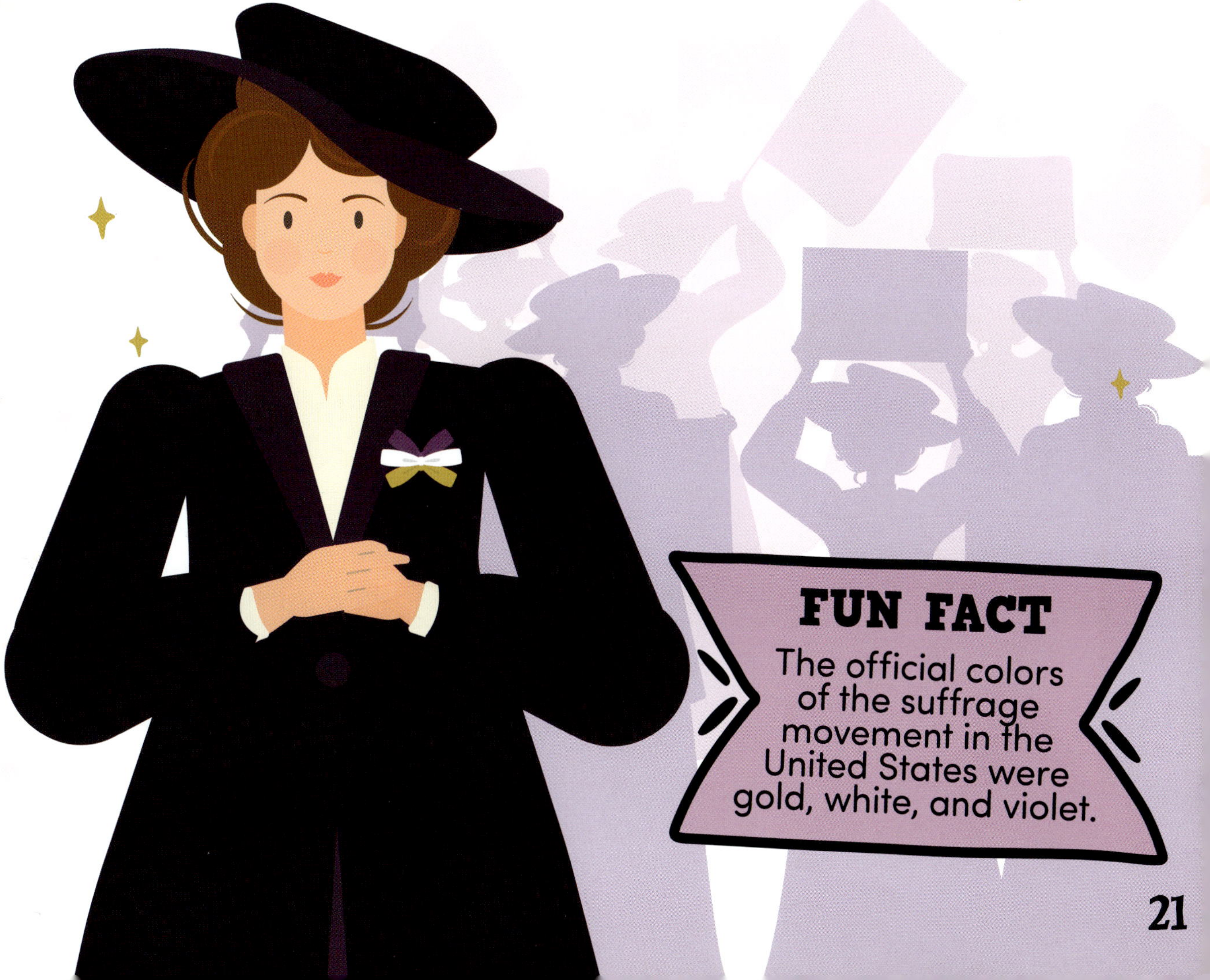

FUN FACT

The official colors of the suffrage movement in the United States were gold, white, and violet.

Asking Questions

This book is full of questions you might have had about history. How do we know the answers? Many people before you have asked the same things.

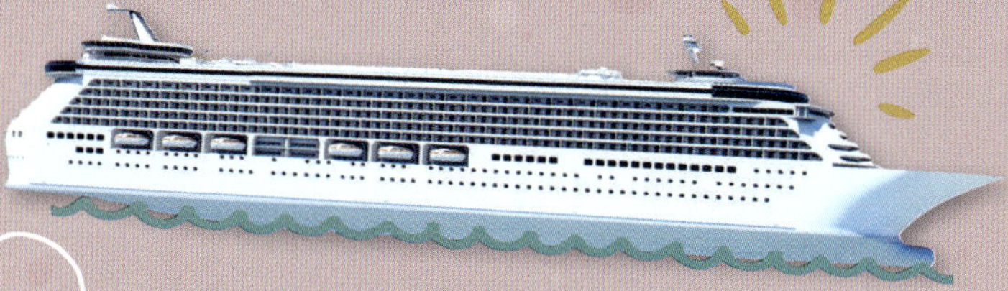

Asking questions is a great way to learn about the world around you. There are still many things to discover about history. So, stay curious, and keep asking questions!

QUESTION

What other questions do you have about history?

Glossary

adjust to get used to something that is different

afterlife the life of a person after they die

emperor the ruler of a large area

eruptions explosions from volcanoes that throw out hot lava and ash with huge force

extinct when a kind of plant or animal has died out completely

germs tiny living things that can cause sickness

invading trying to take over an area

organs parts of the body, such as the lungs or the heart, that do particular jobs

right the permission to be able to do or have something

solved answered a question or problem

symbols pictures or objects that stand for something else

technology the use of science to invent useful tools that do certain things

Index